CW00505572

The Deal Sourcers Toolkit

D. Elawel

As a sourcer this is a comprehensive guide and fantastic toolkit in order to set up a compliant business.
Andrew Tonks - Property Sourcer
AMT Property Sourcing Ltd.

I feel that I could confidently source for investors knowing that I would be compliant using your book.
Karen Meadows – Property Investor. Your Property Options

Having known Dilnashin for nearly 18 months now I can say that she is diligent and particular in her work. I know she has a lot of knowledge in this area and has put a lot of work into this book. It's a fantastic read.
Jo Jamison Da Silva
Flex   Property   Lead   Generation

DEDICATION

To the little people in my life - you have made me stronger and wiser, life would be boring without you.

And to my husband for your consistent encouragement and support. Without you I don't think this Toolkit would have come into being.
Thank you.

.

ACKNOWLEDGMENTS

It was whilst I was attending the annual Property Investors Network (PIN) big event in March called Strategy Implementation Live (SIL) that I had the idea for this book.

I was advising some delegates on how to set up a deal sourcing business and was overheard by my colleague Jo Jamison Da Silva, founder of Flex Property Lead Generation. She advised me that this information is valuable, much needed and I should put it into a book.
I then had my good friends James and Jasmine Rogers of The Fleur Property Group sending delegates to me for further information on this aspect.
I am grateful to you all for your support.

I would also like to thank all the people who I have bounced ideas off and who have encouraged me since I started my deal sourcing journey back in 2019; Hanif Khan, Khalid Mohammed of Attwood Estates and Saj Hussain for his encouragement.

Gwyn Thomas, Karen Meadows, Andrew Tonks, Shehena Chowdhury and Guv Shergill have read snippets of this book and given me great feedback.

1. Introduction

Welcome to the Deal Sourcers Toolkit.

My journey began in late 2018 when I was looking for a source of income that would fit around a young family and without having to commit to going to a physical place of work. At the same time, I was reading a famous book called Rich Dad Poor Dad by Robert Kiyosaki. On my YouTube feed up came a well-known UK property trainer, I watched with intrigue as the strategy of deal sourcing was explained. My passion for property combined with helping people actually seemed possible.

Over the following weeks different property training videos came up on my YouTube feed and I found myself on a webinar by one of the leading UK property trainers. Deal sourcing just seemed to make sense and seemed achievable so I found myself parting with a large sum of money to join a deal sourcing course.

The information provided was good, the support via Facebook (FB) and WhatsApp was great and easy to access. I was happy that being a property sourcer was an achievable path to a good income. The training emphasis was rightly focused on how to source property deals, the most fruitful ways to find deals and advice that sourcing should be done through a limited company.

Then came my stumbling block – setting up a compliant business. This was something that was not discussed in the course, it was touched upon, but not in any depth.

On numerous FB groups and forums, I saw people joining property deal sourcing training programmes, asking the same questions time and again and the answers that were given were often empty and vague. This could land a person in a lot of trouble through no fault of their own despite them trying to get it right.

That was early 2019, and at the time of writing this book in 2020, I see the same questions being asked in the FB groups by a new group of potential deal sourcers.

My nature is such that I like to research, I like to read and get to the bottom of why something has to be done. As I did more research, I found that completing the compliance was not that bad, and I found I knew more than many on the course and others were coming to me for advice. I enjoyed doing the research and putting together the documents, this was probably due to my previous role in operational management and auditing (I secretly love paperwork!).

I felt frustrated that there was no comprehensive (and most importantly) easy to understand guidance out there. I knew that the time and energy I had spent researching and drafting documents is not something that most people would like to do. We join these deal sourcing programmes to show us how to source. And so, because I had spent hours researching and contacting the relevant regulatory bodies for clarification, I decided to create my own guide and document to help others.

You now hold that very guide in your hands. I want readers of this book to feel like they can read it and be empowered with the knowledge and confidence to set up a fully compliant deal sourcing business.

There is no lengthy glossary or appendix at the end, all the information is neatly integrated within the body of the book. Through this book and related articles on the website I aim to add value to your business and make your compliance journey slightly easier.

2. Why I created this book

I am not a property trainer; I am not a tax adviser nor a legally qualified professional. This book is the result of my journey setting up a fully compliant property sourcing business.

As I started my property journey, like many others, I was drawn into the deal sourcing world, told that it can be done part time over a few hours a week (as a mum of young children this appealed to me) and can replace an average salary through a deal or two each month, I jumped at the idea. I was told that there are networks of cash ready, time poor investors waiting for the deals that we as sourcers can bring to the table.

There was advice that setting up as a limited company would be beneficial for tax purposes and that registration with regulatory bodies is required.

However it is not enough just to register with the relevant bodies, you need to know *why* you are required to comply with these bodies and you need to have a procedure in place that helps you/your company ADHERE to the regulations and THAT is why this book has been written.

There are a huge number of property trainers in the market showing novice investors how to become property deal sourcers and make thousands of pounds as a side hustle. What property trainers fail to highlight is the fact that this is not just a side hustle, it must be set up as a real business and comply with the required and relevant UK legislations.

I researched *what* was required to set up a compliant business and *why* this was required, how I should produce my risk assessments and policy documents to ensure I complied with Information Commissioners Office (ICO), The Property Ombudsman (TPO) and Her Majesty's Revenue and Customs (HMRCs) Money Laundering Regulations (MLR) also called Anti Money Laundering (AML).

I found out that it is mandatory for HMRC and ICO registrations to keep accurate training records for the staff in your business. None of this is really discussed in the trainings that I have been part of.

After having purchased ready-made documents supplied by trainers and people in the property sourcing sector, I had the feeling that 'something was still missing', and so I have filled the gaps and simplified the whole process. I have tried to keep this book free from jargon and as simple to understand as possible.

There are a number of books on the subject of property deal sourcing which cover who you need to register with in order to become compliant. There are a few places that offer ready-made documents that you can use for your compliance. And then there is a gap in the middle – you do actually need to know what all the relevant compliance is for, why you are required to comply, and how you need to comply.

It is my aim to give you that information. The information you will require if HMRC knock on your door and ask you to explain what the MLR 2017 requires of your sourcing business and what you have in place to meet those obligations. This is a very important yet overlooked step when setting up as a deal sourcer.

3. What's in this book

When setting up any business there are regulations, every industry has regulations for the protection of its customers and property sourcing is no different, in fact as a property sourcer, for HMRC requirements, we are classed the same as an estate agent and governed by the Estate Agency Act 1979.

I will guide you through the main regulating bodies for deal sourcers, what is required to comply with them, why we need to comply, how to produce the risk assessments and from that the policy documents for your company, and a procedure that you and your staff can follow to comply with your policy. Sounds fun right?

Many people I speak to don't know about this vital part, they are not sure what is involved and even how to start to deal with it. Let me assist you here.

Setting up a business is easy, on the surface, but as you start to see all the regulations around property deal sourcing it starts to look like a can of worms. It takes much research, time and effort to set up the compliance side, and that's even before you have started to look at any properties!

I have found too many property books touch upon an issue regarding compliance, but don't tell you how the writers know this information or why it's important - and so I've included this in for you where it is relevant.

This book covers the most common questions including: which SIC (Standard Industrial Classification) code do I need for deal sourcing? Can training courses be offset as company expenses? Where do I get the policy documents to comply with UK Anti Money Laundering?

The book does not cover strategies, or which strategies you should use for sourcing. I am not telling you which way to steer your business – there are plenty of training providers in the UK who cover that. This book is here to see you through the boring but essential foundation of your business so that you can focus on building relationships, helping people and closing those deals!

4. What is Property Deal Sourcing?

Deal sourcing or becoming a deal sourcer simply means that you are sourcing property for investors, this could be commercial or residential depending on your area of interest. It can either be bespoke for investors or you can source and sell to your list of pre-qualified investors.

You can source from agents; you can source direct to landlords or you can target property owners using social media. There are other tried and tested methods that may have been put in front of you depending on who's course you have attended.

All of these methods can work, as long as you do it correctly and consistently - this is the key to success here.

For example, a poorly written newspaper advert, with no call to action and a mobile contact number that just rings out will never yield results. In addition, we have seen that coloured envelopes that drop onto HMO landlords doormats are now often not opened, landlords are aware that this is unsolicited marketing.

So many trainers have been teaching students to send coloured envelopes but the letters inside are ludicrously poor in content, spelling and grammar.

To be a successful sourcer you also need great planning, marketing and negotiation skills. And often sourcers work alone, so you need to be excellent at time management and self-discipline! And probably more important than all these – you need to have the right mindset, a mindset for success!

Finally, but most importantly, being a property deal sourcer means that you are classed as an Estate Agent and therefore regulated by the Estate Agents Act 1979.

So, if this interests you, if you enjoy interacting with people, love property, love smelly houses and you would like to make a few thousand pounds per deal then read on to find out how to set up your deal sourcing business.

5. Important first steps when setting up your business

After deciding to become a deal sourcer and starting a deal sourcing business, there are a number of fundamental steps you need to carry out before you start trading. The most common ones are listed below.

Decide on a business name, your brand and logo: This is a very important step, so spend time choosing it well, but don't spend weeks doing it. Look at other businesses in the industry and at their branding for inspiration. The main thing here is to 'model' them rather than copy them directly, and to create the impression of a professional organisation.

Even if you are just a single person operating the business, you want a potential client to feel comfortable and confident when interacting with you.

Have a plan: What do you want to achieve in your business, how many deals do you want to source and sell, what will you do with that money? Do you want to purchase your own investment property in the future?

How much you will charge for your deals:
Please work this out carefully and do not just pluck the arbitrary £3,000 - £5,000 per deal that is touted around. Justify what fees your investors are required to pay for your time, experience and expertise.

Take into consideration how much or little time the investor will need to put into the property and what return they will achieve in year 1 and onwards. There are formulas that can be used when pricing up a Rent to Rent deal, when sourcing a property to flip, or a simple buy to let.

Register your UK business: Here you will either use a company set up service to do this for you, which includes registering at Companies House and having a registered office address that is not your home address, or you can register it yourself with the relevant agencies.

Under this subject a whole host of questions arise. At the end of this book I recommend a fantastic FB group which discusses all of this and more.

Be aware of the Standard Industrial Classification (SIC) code: When you register your business Companies House will require you to tell them what activity/activities your business does using codes.

There are a huge number of property related codes, get this right first-time round – SIC 68310 is for property sourcing. This is not the code for flipping, holding or managing property. On an additional note, if you are doing Rent to Rent then the code you will need is 68209.

If you have any doubt here about how to correctly set up your business, please find a property tax accountant – ideally one who is actively investing in property themselves.

Websites, office numbers, call answering services and business cards: All of these add to the credibility of your business.

However – and this is just my personal opinion – before you go out and spend a lot of time and money signing up to these services, do your research and ask yourself if you really need this service right now.

You may set all this up and then not start any marketing for a further 3-6 months, all the while your business expenses are rolling out each month. Think about the plan of action first.

There are recommended companies out there, there are cheap companies, and there are really poor companies who do not provide a good user experience. Go onto the Facebook groups and ask for recommendations and user reviews.

Business bank account: This is very important and you will need this of course. Another common question in the groups is from people struggling to open bank accounts, some banks require lots of proof of what your business will be doing for example.

Some banks ask lots of unnecessary questions and if things are proving difficult during the business account application stage, then it may be a sign that you should look for another provider.

There are the newer and lesser known banks, but be aware that they may not provide client accounts which you need to hold investor funds until the deal is sealed, so please ask this question when looking at which provider to go with.

Now onto the essential 5-point guide covering the compliance required to become a deal sourcer.

6. YOUR 5 points to compliance

6.1 Terms and Conditions of Business

Having a terms and conditions (T&Cs) of business document is vitally important. This sets out the framework in which you will provide your service to your clients. It sets out the boundaries of your service, otherwise your clients may expect more of you than you can deliver, it also limits your liability.

T&Cs also provide assurance to the client that their personal information will be safe with you, what data you will collect and the steps you will take to safeguard it.

It also lets the client know what *they* will have to provide to you, in terms of information (for example the identification documents for your Money Laundering obligations) and assistance in order for you to source for them. Your terms and conditions should also include a disclaimer so that you cannot be held liable for any issues that may arise.

You can put the terms and conditions document on your website if you have one or present it to the client when you meet them. It is very important that they agree to the terms – either by signing the document or some other declaration, otherwise you will not be able to enforce the terms should anything go wrong.

When you first establish your business, you can set up basic T&Cs yourself. As you get to know your business and the types of issues that come up when dealing with clients, you can further refine this document.

Please don't make the mistake of making this document overly complicated and full of jargon. Make it simple and easy to understand, a document that will promote and flourish a successful relationship between you and your client.

6.2 Professional Indemnity and Other Insurances

Why do you need insurance? Every business needs some kind of insurance, as a deal sourcer we will be offering property deals based on our calculations, our assumptions and our due diligence.

Sometimes things can go wrong, perhaps our information is not quite correct, perhaps there are situations that we did not foresee that could cause a financial loss. When investors come to you, they should already know that they want to invest in property.

Ideally, they should already have some investment property. In any case, this is where we would need Professional Indemnity insurance.

Remember that unless you are trained as such, do not offer financial advice to your clients. Only a trained FSA advisor can advise a client on what they should do with their money.

Property business insurance brokers: There are specialist insurance brokers who provide insurance for property deal sourcing, they know the business and what you will be doing, so their registration is very simple.

Do not make the mistake that I did when dealing with my first broker – they provided me with a 20-page document full of questions about me, my business, what I would be doing and lots of questions that I didn't even understand let alone know the answers to.

All of these things produce unnecessary stress when you are in the initial stage of your business. If the process is unduly complicated, then my advice would be to move onto another provider.

Look in the property FB groups to find recommendations of service providers. At the time of writing this book the annual cost is around £270 for £500,000 of PI cover.

Vehicle insurance: If you are using your own vehicle for your business, for example if you are driving to viewings and/or to meet clients, then you will need to update your vehicle insurance with your current provider to cover business use.

6.3 Property Ombudsman Scheme

In 2007 the Consumers Estate Agents and Redress Act 2007 made it mandatory for agents to belong to an ombudsman. The term ombudsman is used to describe a person who is appointed to investigate complaints made against a company.

None of us go into business thinking that anyone will make a complaint against us, or that we may fail to deliver on a contract. This scheme is here to protect us as businesses as well as our clients.

There are currently 2 government approved redress schemes, these are The Property Ombudsman (TPO) and The Property Redress Scheme (PRS).

www.tpos.co.uk

www.theprs.co.uk

TPO

TPO is a not-for-profit independent company, it has 9 Non-Executive Directors who appoint the Ombudsman. They have two levels that a sourcer can join, both at the same price; *Registration only*, which requires us to follow the TPO's General Membership Obligations and have use of the 'Approved Redress Scheme' sign.

The other option is to join the *Full Membership* in which you agree to follow their Codes of Practice and you can display the blue TPO sign (as you may have seen in many estate agents' windows).

The TPO provide a number of booklets that you can give to your clients to explain what the code of conduct is and they also provide the window stickers that you need to display outside your business.

At the time of writing this book, June 2020, the current cost of registering with the TPO for both schemes is the same, as follows;

Registration only and Full Membership Prices;

Registration £60 + Vat
Annual fee £225 + Vat

This includes a fair usage policy that covers up to 3 ombudsman supported claims per year and then £350+vat for every subsequent claim that is brought against you/your business.

Personally, I registered with the TPO, I like their code of conduct guidelines, the registration was very easy and I found their customer service to be very good.

PRS
Next let's look at the PRS.

PRS is a subsidiary of an insurance services company. They are a profit-making company. PRS do not have any set code of conduct but rather they expect you/your business to have a code of good practice for your business.

They have 2 membership options;

Entry Model
£110 +Vat per application
£100 +Vat for each complaint made against your business.

Enhanced Model
£199 + Vat per application
No complaint fee (subject to a fair usage policy)

I have not used the PRS but I do know of many colleagues in the industry who do and they have no problem. In addition to this when I have contacted the PRS I have always found their email response time and customer service to be good.

Your own complaints procedure
It is very important to note that although you need to register with one of the above schemes, your client cannot use them to settle a dispute until they have exhausted your own *in-house complaints procedure.*

This is a simple document to produce, every good business that has confidence in its ability should really show the client the complaints procedure along with their terms and conditions of business.

Your complaints procedure should outline who the point of contact is within your company for complaints and ow a complaint should be made by the client.

It should outline what the time frame is for the complaint to be addressed, both in the first instance of acknowledging the complaint and then investigating the complaint.

Ultimately, if the client is still not happy with the outcome you provide there must be the option of taking the issue to the ombudsman that you are registered with.

6.4 The Information Commissioners Office (ICO)

www.ico.org.uk

ICO Registration Cost: The current registration fee for the ICO is £40 per year, if you pay by direct debit this amount will be reduced to £35 per year.

What is the ICO?
The ICO is a regulatory body which upholds information rights in the public interest, it ensures that public bodies are transparent and data protection of individuals is honoured.

Because we are collecting, processing and storing data about our clients, the people that we meet and the communications that we have, we are required to register and comply with the ICO.

Any information that we hold about an individual has to be kept safe, we must only collect and keep what is necessary and we must dispose of that information after the relevant time period.

The ICO is responsible for enforcing and promoting compliance with the General Data Protection Regulation (GDPR), the Data Protection Act (DPA) 2018 and other legislation. Section 146 of the DPA 2018 gives them power to conduct compulsory audits to ensure that businesses are compliant with these regulations.

All companies and organisations who collect information about individuals have to comply with the UK Data Protection Act 2018, along with the GDPR, which also forms part of UK law.

As a deal sourcer we will undoubtedly be collecting and holding information about our investors. We may be collecting and processing information about landlords and therefore we are bound by this legislation.

The GDPR came into effect on 25th May 2018. It sets out the main principles, rights and obligations for most processing of personal data. The ICO puts the onus on you as a business to assess how and why you use the data that you collect.

The ICO and Risk Assessment for your business

You have to be able to justify to the ICO why you are collecting, how you are using, and why you are keeping the data. You have to show how you are keeping it safe and this will be highlighted to you when you do a risk assessment to identify where the potential gaps are in your business.

ICO have some guidance on the definitions of different areas of data, things they believe are important, and an example of a breech so you can see how things could spiral out of control if you don't take care. I have included these here so that you can include them in your risk assessment:

- **Personal Data** – this is information about a living individual, any information that could enable someone to identify who a person is by their full name, home address, date of birth, bank details etc.
- **Processing** – anything that you do with the data including collecting, recording, storing, analysing and deleting.

- **Controller** – this is the person who decides how and why to collect and use this data. The controller could be a sole trader, a director, but could also be an employee in an organisation. It is the controller who must make sure that the data complies with the law.
- **Processor** – this is a separate person or organisation who processes the data on behalf of the controller.
- **Data Subject** – this is the term for the individual who we collect the data about.

Your risk assessment should ideally be a walk-through of how data goes through your business and then highlight all the points where an incident could occur. Once these have been identified, you will then be able to put into place the measures to ensure that incidences do not occur.

From the risk assessment above you will then be able to compile your data protection policy and data handling policy.

Data Protection Policy: You will need a data protection policy for your business, this will outline how you collect the data, what data you keep, the type of data and if you will share the data. Indicate if this data is sensitive in any way. You need to explain to your clients how you will use their data.

Data Handling Policy: The data handling policy accompanies the data protection policy. This is the document which sets out the day to day procedures that staff must adhere to with relation to the data that is coming through the business.

The data protection policy and data handling policy are both internal business documents. Once you have completed a data risk assessment you will have a better idea of how to form your policy.

On the ICO website they have examples of data breaches and what consequences this may have on the parties involved. Use this information to help you understand how you may think of any gaps in your business data handling.

1. **Training Log:** It is also very important to have a training log for ICO. This sets out how you will cover the responsibility of safe data handling with your staff. This document should be signed and dated by the individual staff members.

Privacy Policy: If you have a website then you will need to have a Privacy Policy displayed on your website. This tells your visitors how you will collect data from their visit and what you will do with that data.

This is especially relevant if you have a contact form where visitors will enter and submit their data to you. The privacy policy is an external business document.

Customer Relationship Management System: Most businesses use a Customer Relationship Management (CRM) system for data and information in the business. You must make sure that the system you are using is secure, encrypted and has a backup. There are a number of good CRMs on the market, ensure that it meets your needs and will keep your data safe.

6.5 HMRC's Anti Money Laundering (AML)

www.gov.uk/guidance/register-or-renew-your-money-laundering-supervision-with-hmrc

Money laundering and the property business

In June 2017 the Money Laundering, Terrorist Financing and Transfer of Funds Regulations (MLR) 2017 came into effect. This legislation outlines what obligations are required on businesses that deal in areas considered to be at high risk of exposure to criminals laundering money.

The MLR put strict obligations on businesses and individuals to conduct tighter levels of due diligence on their clients, identify the true beneficial owner in a transaction and the source of the funds to help reduce the risk of your business being used as a vehicle for laundering money.

Money laundering is essentially the cleaning of dirty money. Criminals look to 'clean' money that has been obtained from criminal activities.

This is often done by setting up various companies which link together, the money moves from one company to another and then used to purchase high value items such as property, art, vehicles and jewellery, amongst other things.

Property is high value in certain parts of the country, meaning more money can be put into what looks like a legitimate asset. It is held for a few years and then sold to release the 'clean' money.

The Financial Action Task Force (FATF) is a global authority and standard setter in the area of money laundering and counter terrorist financing.

The UK is governed by the FATFs guidelines and in December 2018 the UK was praised for having the strongest AML regime out of over 60 countries.

FATF has identified that there are 3 stages in money laundering.
Firstly, the dirty money is PLACED into the financial system, this could be through deposits into bank accounts or purchasing treasury bills, for example.

Secondly the money is LAYERED, meaning it is moved to different accounts or used to purchase goods or services. For example, this illicit money could be used to set up a legitimate 'cash only' business.

Thirdly INTEGRATION, this is the point where the funds are used to purchase property or luxury goods with the seemingly clean cashflow from the business.

So, you can see how important it is to establish the true source of funds that your investor is intending to use.

Either or both parties in a transaction (seller and/or buyer) could be trying to launder money.

Companies, parent companies, foreign companies, etc can all be set up and linked with each other to hide the true original source of funds. And so, we need strict measures in place to protect ourselves.

The UK government produced a campaign called 'Flag It Up' (**https://flagitup.campaign.gov.uk/**) to highlight the importance of this issue and how we should try to protect ourselves. This is an interesting document and provides lots of insight to money laundering.

According to the National Crime Agency (NCA) the laundering of dirty money is estimated annually to be hundreds of billions of pounds in the UK. NCA is involved in investigating and reducing serious organized crime which is fuelled by laundered money.

Property sourcers are regulated and supervised by HMRC because they come under the Estate Agency Act. The estate agency business is regulated under section 1 of the Estate Agency Act 1979.

A property sourcer is classed as medium risk by the UKs 2nd national risk assessment of Money Laundering Regulations published in October 21017. The UK's HMRC is responsible for ensuring all businesses who fall under Estate Agency are registered and comply with the Money Laundering Regulations 2017.

AML Supervision

When you apply for your AML supervision there are a number of parts and associated fees to the process (correct at time of print):

- **Registering Your Business Premises:** There is an annual fee of £300 for each business premises that you register in your application.
- **Fit and Proper Test:** There is the Fit and Proper Test for each person involved in the business at a one-off fee of £150 for each person.
- **Approval Fee:** An annual approval fee of £40 per person is also applied to estate agency businesses.

You can check the related HMRC webpage below for the latest fees:

https://www.gov.uk/guidance/money-laundering-regulations-registration-fees

Fit and proper test

The fit and proper test needs to be carried out on all persons who are registering and will be running the business. It includes company directors and senior managers. HMRC will check that you are a responsible and capable person in regards to money laundering.

HMRC will check if you have previously been convicted of money laundering or fraudulent activities and if you have been disqualified from a previous post as a director. HMRC will also do an approval test on you.

They will carry out these checks using government and law enforcement bodies as well as other regulatory bodies.

In order to comply with HMRCs AML, your business needs to have an assessment of the risks facing it, policy documents for your business, and a procedure for your business to follow.

You will also need to have a Client Due Diligence (CDD or KYC) checklist in place and you need to know what a Suspicious Activity Report (SAR) is and how to file one should you need to – more is explained about these later.

AML policy

Every deal sourcer I speak to who knows about needing to become compliant will say that they need to have an AML policy in place, and the next question is "where can I get a copy of this?"

What trainers and people/places who sell these policy documents fail to tell you is that it is not just the simple issue of buying a document that says 'AML Policy' on it.

There is actually a whole process that you need to go through with regard to AML and complying with the Money Laundering Regulations 2017, and the policy document is the bit in the middle of this process.

Risk Assessment of your business

Policy produced from the Risk Assessment

Procedures for your staff and company created as a result of the policy document

As you can see from the diagram above; you cannot just purchase a policy document off the shelf and expect it to meet the needs of your business.

Over the next few pages, we will break down each of these parts and help you apply them to your business. This will enable you to create your own policy document.

Only you know how you will conduct your business and the risks that you will face. Also, by creating your own risk assessment you will understand the process and be able to explain your understanding of the MLR 2017 and how they apply to your business to HMRC if and when they knock on your door.

AML Risk Assessment

What is a risk?

"The possibility of something bad happening at some point in the future; a situation that could be dangerous or have a bad result" *Oxford Advanced Learners Dictionary*

What is a risk assessment?

"The act of identifying possible risks, calculating how likely they are to happen and estimating what effects they may have. . ." *Oxford Advanced Learners Dictionary*

Using the Money Laundering Regulations 2017 we can see there are specific areas that we need to look at; Here is section 18 of the MLR 2017;

"Risk assessment by relevant persons
18.— (1) A relevant person must take appropriate steps to identify and assess the risks of money
laundering and terrorist financing to which its business is subject.
(2) In carrying out the risk assessment required under paragraph (1), a relevant person must take into account—
(a) information made available to them by the supervisory authority under regulations 17(9) and 47, and

(b) risk factors including factors relating to—
(i) its customers;

(ii) the countries or geographic areas in which it operates;
(iii) its products or services;
(iv) its transactions; and
(v) its delivery channels.

(3) In deciding what steps are appropriate under paragraph (1), the relevant person must take into account the size and nature of its business.
(4) A relevant person must keep an up-to-date record in writing of all the steps it has taken under paragraph (1), unless its supervisory authority notifies it in writing that such a record is not required.
(5) A supervisory authority may not give the notification referred to in paragraph (4) unless it considers that the risks of money laundering and terrorist financing applicable to the sector in which the relevant person operates are clear and understood.
(6) A relevant person must provide the risk assessment it has prepared under paragraph (1), the information on which that risk assessment was based and any record required to be kept under paragraph (4), to its supervisory authority on request."

Breaking down the above legislation we can see that it must be a senior and relevant person who carries out the risk assessment.

You should have 5 headings on your assessment detailing the risk areas given above and then what measures you will put in place to mitigate these risks.

For example, if we look at delivery channels – how do you intend to do business? Will it be face to face or virtually, will you be dealing with people who are based within or outside the UK? If you are dealing with the latter there will be increased risk, how will you reduce that risk upon your business?

Verifying your clients and customers

If we look at who your customer is, also known as **Know Your Customer (KYC)** – you need to identify if they are an individual or a business.

If they are an individual you must verify their identity using Gov.uk guidelines.

Are they considered to be a PEP (politically exposed person), are they linked to a high-risk country or have financial sanctions on them?

You must also be able to verify the funds that they have allocated for your product or service.

There is guidance available on how to check identification documents on the following webpage;

https://www.gov.uk/government/publicatio ns/identity-proofing-and-verification-of-an-individual/identity-proofing-and-verification-of-an-individual

There are also a number of companies that you can sign up to who will do these background checks for you. The fees vary for these services, but please remember that you are ultimately still responsible so you may need to do your own checks as well.

If an investor is not willing to cooperate and give you information on ID verification, then they could be hiding something. On a side note please be aware that this information will probably not be something that will be given up on a first meeting.

You first need to establish a rapport, identify if you can help this investor with what they require and then obtain all the verification information you need before any property deals are discussed.

Your risk assessment and company policy
Do not think that your risk assessment needs to be a long and complicated, jargon filled document. It needs to be an easy to understand, easy to administer document that you will follow with each investor/buyer/vendor that you work with.

A simple, attractive document that you can build upon will get more use than a complicated one.

From your risk assessment you will be able to identify how you think you should mitigate the risks.

The risk assessment will form the foundation of your policy, this must be an evolving process, you must update your risk assessment at least annually so that you can be sure your policy document is always current and relevant.

AML Policy Document

What is a policy?

"A course or principle of action adopted or proposed by an organisation or individual"
Oxford Dictionary

As a deal sourcer you need to have policy documents in place which outline what your company position is in relation to the required guidelines and how you will proceed to meet that expectation.

A good policy document should be easily available to use and understand. For example, going back to how you will deliver your services as a deal sourcer – 'XYZ Ltd will only deal with investors based in the UK'. This is an example of company policy statement.

Company procedure documents

Moving forward from this you need to compile a procedure document. A procedure is exactly what it says – it is a step by step guide for staff to follow when dealing with clients. When a new member of staff joins your company the training they receive will be from these procedure documents.

Carrying on from our example above – if a foreign investor shows an interest in your sourcing services, you/your staff will know by your company policy that you cannot deal with them. The customer can then be informed of that policy.

In addition to these documents you will also need to have client due diligence forms. There are two versions that you will need to produce; a Basic Due Diligence sheet and an Enhanced Due Diligence sheet. This check is also known as **Know Your Customer.**

Basic client due diligence checklist: This check sheet should cover information such as the customer's name, address and date of birth.
It should be verified by official government issued photographic identification.

Again, remember that even if you outsource this checking to an independent company, you are still liable if that company does not check accurately.

If you have a situation where the **beneficial owner** has a representative, you must ensure you are able to verify identity without any undue obstacles.

For example, an elderly parent may own a property but its being sold through a child, you must clearly see the relationship and know that permission comes from the beneficial owner not the representative.

Enhanced customer due diligence: This is required when your client poses a higher risk of money laundering. This could be for example if they are from or linked to high risk countries.

It may be that they are a Politically Exposed Person (PEP) or have close links to a PEP, the MLR requires enhanced due diligence in this situation. The UK HM Treasury website has a list that you can refer to for information on PEPs and high-risk countries.

Both basic and enhanced client due diligence is an ongoing process that needs to be reviewed at regular intervals to make sure that nothing has changed for the individual or business. It is very important that all records are kept for 5 full years after the end of your business relationship with the client. This data has to be kept safe, encrypted and offsite.

Visit our website to see what checklists we offer to support your business www.DealSourcersToolkit.com

Suspicious Activity Report (SAR)

Another important issue to be aware of is how to raise a Suspicious Activity Report (SAR).

As a deal sourcer you will have contact with lots of different people. If you feel that any customer is behaving suspiciously – for example they want to do a transaction with a large amount of cash or you feel that they are not being transparent and forthcoming with information. In this case the Nominated Officer in your business should be informed and then they can decide if there is enough reason to file a SAR to the National Crime Agency (NCA).

Nominated Officer

Having a Nominated Officer is a requirement of the MLR regulations. If you are a single person business then you as director will need to take on that role.

It is important to note that as a senior member (director etc) of a business regulated by HMRC you are personally liable if you do not set up your business correctly to protect against being used for money laundering.

The UK government is under pressure to plug the gaps in the economy which are exploited by criminals. In turn HMRC are putting increased pressure on all business where money laundering can occur.

HMRC have a number of penalties that they can use if you/your business fails to comply with the regulations. However please be aware that these measures are there to encourage you to comply with the regulations rather than threaten with prison/fines.

Training log

Lastly but also very importantly you will need a training log to show what training has been done and when.

This is very important as you may be asked by HMRC to show the level of knowledge and compliance that staff within your business have. Training must be done at regular intervals and especially when there are updates in the industry or in the legislation.

If you enjoy reading, there are a number of GOV.UK publications on money laundering and risk assessments, one example is below;
https://assets.publishing.service.gov.uk/go vernment/uploads/system/uploads/attachm ent_data/file/655198/National_risk_assessm ent_of_money_laundering_and_terrorist_fi nancing_2017_pdf_web.pdf

Information on penalties that can be issued by HMRC for non-compliance;
https://www.gov.uk/guidance/money-laundering-regulations-appeals-and-penalties.

7. Other Important Issues Related to Deal Sourcing

On the following pages you will find various issues relating to a sourcing business, some are in heated discussions at the time of writing this book, others I hope you will find beneficial for your journey.

The Issue of Co-Sourcing

Over the space of nearly two years I have seen the issue of co-sourcing come up often. Co-sourcing is where you source property or investors, without being compliant yourself, and then sell/pass them onto another company which is registered as compliant. You then get paid a commission for your services.

Now some people say that this is illegal and it breaks certain rules and regulations. However, they do not say what regulations are broken here.

Looking at this from a logical perspective, if you are supplying **leads** to any company for a payment, it is up to the receiving company to carry out proper verification and due diligence on the lead.

Just as a compliant sourcer would have to investigate the source of funds or property being offered – which is part of the AML requirements. The supplying co-sourcer is not registered as part of your business, other than the commission you will pay them for the lead, they have no contract with your business.

So, taking all this into account, and this is entirely my opinion, there is nothing wrong if you choose not to register as a compliant property sourcer but rather choose to generate leads for a compliant company.

However, you must make it contractually clear that you are only providing leads, and all due diligence and AML requirements are entirely the responsibility of the compliant registered business who are receiving them.

Dealing with the expense of a course

Can training courses be offset against your income? Now I am not an accountant or any kind of financial advisor but this question comes up time and again and incorrect answers are always thrown around.

When I did my first property course, I was told in the training that the cost of the course could be offset as a business expense.

Towards the end of my first year of trading I looked into this further, the information in the groups is very contradicting and so it is best to seek advice from an accountant.

However, I consulted the HMRC Business Income Manual which gives detailed guidance on this issue. The bottom line here is that if this is your first ever training in a new area then it is more for your personal development than a business expense and cannot be claimed back.

Any subsequent training and development can be classed as an expense because you are continuing your development in that area and that will in turn benefit the business. But again, please seek advice from a qualified professional.

Networking
Networking is very important in the property industry. The saying 'people buy from people who they know, like and trust' is so true.

In this industry there are large sums of money and lots of risk involved, therefore if you want people to give you money for sourcing, they have to firstly know they can trust you and secondly, like you, your ethics, and how you do your business.

It is always helpful to have a small portfolio of your deals, the properties that you view, costs of conversion and expected monthly profits.

Even if these deals never go through, you can still show investors that you know how to stack a deal. You can show that you are aware of refurbishment costs, returns expected in the area and other points. Please be truthful and do not attempt to hide information. This is all about building your credibility with your business.

I was very grateful to have been asked to be a part of the team at my local Property Investors Network (PIN) meeting back in 2019. I find these meetings a valuable way to keep your momentum going when starting out. Surrounding yourself with likeminded people, immersing yourself in knowledge of the industry and listening to real life case studies all strengthen belief in your goal.

PIN meetings are filled with a mixture of experience and novice delegates. You will find business people with money to invest but no property knowledge and seasoned investors.

The key to successfully networking starts with having a plan, identify what you want to achieve from the meeting – do you want to learn something specific, do you want to find a tradesperson, are you looking for a mentor?

And when you are there always start by introducing yourself and then ask about the other person. Find a small way to add value to that person, give a nugget of knowledge or direction to a source of information, you never know that may be the start of a great relationship.

Then most importantly MOVE ON quickly to another person. The point of the event is to meet as many people as you can, do not get stuck with one person, politely move away. If you find someone who you really want to get to know, take their business card and arrange a coffee meeting.

If you have not attended a PIN meeting before, they have 49 meetings each month in locations from Edinburgh to Bournemouth. If you visit PIN at

www.propertyinvestorsnetwork.co.uk/ meetings

You will be able to view the forthcoming meetings and find your local meeting. The meetings usually have a mortgage update as well as real case studies. Each month there is also a substantial prize draw given away at each of the 49 meetings.

As an additional gift to you for purchasing this book – if you have not yet attended a PIN meeting, attend your first meeting using the link below – you or a friend can come for free!

https://is.gd/u6Ityl

Come on – what are you waiting for? You never know who you may meet there.

I have met some great people through these events who have directed and advised me. Made some amazing friends and business partners as well.

Business Cards

Business cards are a must have before you attend any kind of meeting. It makes you look so much more professional if you can pull out a card rather than scrambling for a pen and paper to leave your details.

Facebook

Another way to establish yourself and grow your brand is through using Facebook. By joining various groups, you can learn a wealth of information, however, be sure to do your due diligence on the so-called established property investors who are posting information and guidance. Take your knowledge from an established source.

Parting Advice

I do hope you have found this book useful as you start out on your property deal sourcing business. Compliance is so often a subject that is overlooked, very little support is provided, and yet it is so important to get right from the start.

There are a number of Facebook groups for people in property, all provide good information for those who are new to the industry.

I will say that the Property Newbies FB group provides a wealth of resources and information for everyone. There are lots of 'newbies' in the group as well as experienced property investors who provide help and support.

People in that group have paid for courses, they can advise which are worth it and which not, they have knowledge of different mentors and importantly which ones to stay away from.

I really appreciate you purchasing this guide and I hope it was helpful. You can download a business checklist of all the above points from our website below.

Wishing you a successful property journey!

Please visit us at the website below; www.DealSourcersToolkit.Com

You will find a number of documents to support your business set up as well as articles and information on deal sourcing in general.

Printed in Great Britain
by Amazon